thousands

Also by Lightsey Darst

DANCE
Find the Girl

thousands —————— *poems*

Lightsey Darst

COFFEE HOUSE PRESS

Minneapolis

2017

Coffee House Press books are available to the trade through our primary distributor, Consortium Book Sales & Distribution, cbsd.com or (800) 283-3572. For personal orders, catalogs, or other information, write to info@coffeehousepress.org.

Coffee House Press is a nonprofit literary publishing house. Support from private foundations, corporate giving programs, government programs, and generous individuals helps make the publication of our books possible. We gratefully acknowledge their support in detail in the back of this book.

LIBRARY OF CONGRESS CATALOGING-IN-PUBLICATION DATA

Names: Darst, Lightsey.
Title: Thousands / Lightsey Darst.
Description: Minneapolis : Coffee House Press, 2017.
Identifiers: LCCN 2017012424 | ISBN 9781566894920
    (paperback)
Subjects: | BISAC: POETRY / American / General.
Classification: LCC PS3604.A79 A6 2017 | DDC 811/.6—dc23
LC record available at https://lccn.loc.gov/2017012424

PRINTED IN THE UNITED STATES OF AMERICA

24 23 22 21 20 19 18 17   1 2 3 4 5 6 7 8

thousands

1   **Minneapolis, Minnesota**

to 10/31/11

"The love of my life died in a motorcycle crash"
her words went through me like a needle through tulle
(now she has three children

tenure, a husband, a tolerably well-furnished house).

The student writes,
The weeding is an important day in everyone's life.

"I'd kill for love   Chromatics
kill for la a uv"

Dear what I'll do,

We are all familiar with terror.

This produces the coming catastrophe
of mind or contagion; produces the cloud,
crowd's roil overturning,

this discipline of questions. They don't read, they don't know—
the students,

lovers of terror,
voters, taxpayers,

Notes on
a lecture,
1/19/11

anonymous commenters, ex-soldiers, future mothers,
    fellow citizens, customers of cable television,

to read

In Parenthesis

Felt through my hair for the missing comb. Kept counting
    three, knew
there were four. The blind side feels for itself.

I lost it again—that clump of tulips I never remember to divide,
roots grown thick like a witch's hand.

Every night your voice follows me into sleep
I dream you're yelling at me.

The door is cracked a foot from the top,
as if it broke when you slammed it;
it was broken when we moved in.

Oh you're not that bad a man
I'm not that bad a bitch.

But I have the look of the unloved wife
and you don't know it but everywhere I go
men buy me drinks and hope.

Keep the cat happy and the door shut tight.
Don't forget sight is not the same as a path   2/21/11

Dear good advice,

People gave me directions and I followed them. That's how
    I was then.
"Love—that'll come and go." A summer in Prague
J.   (together walking all day every day)
means nothing. "What are you doing with your life?" So I
A.   married him.

(But I will always know you
walking up the last hill
J.   in your secondhand shirt.)

Well thunder, well lightning,
ring grown loose on my finger

Should have been the world's bride
before I made that vow

Had the beautiful right there and turned it around
to see what was written on the other side.

Open your eyes to see.   4/14/11

On the sidewalk by the lake
crashed shell of a swan, no it's a snake, you can tell
by his soft hollow leather.

Snake eggs, robin eggs, shark case or mermaid's purse,
every kind of closure I kept.

Slipper shell curved where she hugged the back of her host.

I don't know what I have to do

I don't have to do what I do.

Don't mend it. Cold wind comes in & I
don't want to go home—freezes the lake below it in a flat sheet.

Don't ever want to go home.

Look I'm tired of not knowing my way

whether it's left at the light or three jiggers
(you repeat these things as if I should know) I don't want

fastened to dead weight,
I can go on giving you more but no I don't know that. I can't

help you through this let me go let me let me

help. I have to wait or I need more or

I've underestimated what cold is or distance or

dregs dried to the cup it's after six & I
said I'd be home, I have the strength, have the heart after all, so

I have to do it and I have to do it alone.

Desire & the page felt it.
I told myself, something is happening.
I could make weather happen then.

Dear not only in dream life, dear never until storm.

A roomful of people five years younger, their flat sequin eyes.

I knew no one was listening, I needed to protect myself
so I used the past tense.

Watched lovers. No one in their twenties
thought they would have kids or die, but then they did. No
    one knew
what I did. No one was the same.

I gave another dime to the cause, I decided to assist in a birth.

I plumbed the wound with a plait,
I felt how deep it would go.

Dear darkness, dear salt & sugar.
Dear future forest.

I saw myself getting old before my time so I thought about love.

You told me the magic and I listened with my face turned up
J.   to you
lost in the shining brass of the bar.

Come home to our garage, our gate into our garden,
A.   our little house
we painted pine green.

"Do you love him too?" "Yes."

I said, "Leaving you
would be the worst thing I've ever done."

A sparrow bleats into still, caught in a string on our birch.
After eight years' silence, the charm hums on my chest.

Wearing my wedding ring only to take it off.
I could, as early as tomorrow, make everything right.

On Nicollet Avenue the lamps come on
gingkos' lichened, lime-dappled trunks, primeval.

8/17/11
Spyhouse

Enters in the manner of a beautiful woman
so bored with her good marriage.

To make impossibly neat marks. To appear from thin air.
    To summon
from a distance. To make love to one
thinking of another.

Can anything be made better by trying
And I did try hard.

I Want To See You   J.

Risk of history—
rain on the horizon.

Dear scissors gnawing through my hair,
dear think on it

Dear I thought enough

Then I became cruel, or others thought so,

I became quick to cross town ahead
of the moving van, my cat on the seat beside me.

Picked up, drained off my last glass of wine, set off
and my wine glass was the one thing I broke.

2   **Minneapolis, Minnesota**

11/1/11 to summer 2012

The last flower has opened on the stem,
the first two mostly done by now: call home.

I slipped my skin
walked off & left myself & left

feeling the first snow of the season falling
cold on my face running to catch that downtown bus leaving

my life behind & abandoned my whole self, was I
a colt or a fresh coal afire each chain of nerve

alive naked & loving the feeling of feeling
my heart beating feeling my blood too feeling

Dear Wednesday, 7:13 a.m.,

We were owned by each other at that time.

I loved you then, I love you now—the earth is what's moving.

And I enjoyed an excess of everything, surplus shine. Others
     bathed in it,
washed their cold hands.

In bed counting dawn-invisible stars. There was a lot of talk,
the usual kind of talk,

storm, then clear dawn & another near miss.

(Over a stolen cup of wine I conjure this,
light in the clouds late autumn maples,
the magic hour.)

Healthy & wealthy and we went out in bad weather
because we weren't afraid—
oh but this is the present.

Does it, I suppose, go on forever? Yesterday
we named our children.

I got tired of not having sex, you know?
But I don't believe a public private life is a revolutionary act.
    I believe

(haunts the liquor store)   11/29/11

I like my looks. How we fucked last night.
How "fucked" now means just that. A cotangle of intimate hair.
    Fucking,
fuckt.

I don't believe I do have anything to tell you, officer.

How is my business?
(raises an arm, sniffs)

Dear yes,

I had ways

Flouncing along the sidewalk
a trio of girls, no more than fifteen, with round rouged cheeks
    & kissy mouths.

They certainly are beautiful, but not like me.

to read   *Against Expression*
Rae Armantrout:

each poem is a self-contained philosophical exposition, like a
    thirty-something man.

Emily believed in beauty. She believed in handwriting, &
    readers. "Please

Gorgeous   accept a hummingbird."
Nothings

Want to share a pastry? I want half and your fingers sticky,
I want to be your flurry, baby.

12 p.m. & already I miss the feeling of riding—
so dull not to be loved when one can be!

You said, let's see the six tallest buildings in the world
I said I've seen one

Dear why and dearer winter,
dear how and dearer hour.

A thought of you comes to me at every second step, how
the following leg joins me. Is me.

We almost came with our clothes on
voices passing politely in the hall.

I touch your arm to be part of your reading; so's the snow.

"I felt myself to be one thing"; I feel myself to be one thing   Kincaid

climbing down from the silent years.

Oh I should have left when the bridge fell.

Have I said anything yet that's a net to catch you

I've lured a wild animal into my bed. Velvet
moves over the pulse
I can barely stand to see, to know
you're mortal.

Arm bent at the elbow, fingers thread through your
    woodgrain hair that moment before
you wake. I listen for your assertive sleep-sounds, your "Hmm"
    & basso profundo "muh."

Susan Sontag,
*Reborn:
Journals and
Notebooks,
1947–1963*
"I rejoice, that I'm not busy dying—I'm still busy being born."

Aftermath of satiety, the cat licking the blinds again.

I'm not a scholar. If I get a Ph.D. it'll be on my terms, first
    person singular.

"acts of loving description"
with my hands, your tongue, with both our mouths.

When my eyes meet yours
we tell the story again.

Oh that's right, I teach tomorrow—shit

How Sally moves in Jen's ballet, somehow Weimar. dance notes
The history of pointe; Judson Church; exits + entrances;
    eros. to research

(You can go on grading freshman comp in every free hour but
    as for me,
I don't want to die.

Imagine being Lauren Bacall, not seventeen
but you are; you are.)

I came through the linen curtain into the dark alcove where you

lay; touching your face, your clavicle, your sleep-arched cock

achingly I confirmed the shapes of things

A. Cold & cut off from the motion of the heart that used to be mine

—a figure of speech; as we prove,
all property, even that given in love,
2/18/12   is alienable.

Even the wedding photographs can be thrown out without a word.

Maybe I remember them all anyway.

[leaning on your/his arm to fix my high
heeled gold shoe]

I heard of you in grief & compared
what I heard with sunlight coming in through my solo window
        & was

unmoved, or only slightly moved—

murmuring a little benison then turning aside to make these
        neat marks
then ever neater ones on my white blank.

After she left him, he burned in a hotel fire
trying to save his "papers."

Mary
McCarthy

This girl wears her hair up like an old woman
which is cute but why take the risk

And she wouldn't have gone in to save him if she could
because that's what divorce means.

I become more myself this way, wearing
silk over wool over silk like cunt layers. I lift
another lid from my eye.

Freedom, not to say anarchy

moans her answer to her friend, a plate of flan half-eaten

the dim possibility that overall these poems might be too
personal

Spyhouse   I just finished reading that novel you love,
Hennepin

the one with all the fucking, then
disaster, then suddenly everyone is older,
ordinary, then the stage is cleared, in which case

you and I can start over from right now.

Came without moving in the manner of sun or spring or spring

flowers; I point out white violets
you note the contradiction . . . That's you—
timing the moment of touching my thigh
while turning a page without looking, sly.

That scent again of sandalwood soaked in ancient honey, honey—
is that the inside of my wrist
or the dream?

Do you keep a journal
why / why not

Keep one now
keep me in it

Tired of any voice higher than yours = must stay home all day.

You know this way better than anyone,
under the bridges & beyond the arsenal.

I keep waiting for you to bite my neck
gently as a lioness lifts her cub.

That will happen
Everything will happen now.

This is not nighttime is it? —I love that word, with its double
     fence you cross.

Barbette
3/21/12

This Cubist bathroom, not the best place to check your lipstick.

My student Madeleine, Francophile in a Breton top,
seats people at the bar, too young to pour them wine.

Does this endless mirroring
degrade or do you go on being more
& more of perfect, splendid you?

Twenty, then twenty-four, then true love.
Then twenty-nine, thirty-three. I'm vulnerable

to votive flame, figures
passing beyond the window in the rain.

My smeared mouths speak soundlessly, parting & meeting;
beloved, someone's beloved, please keep warmer with your
        collar up.

"Heather. Anna. Leon. Nick." I want a flame, a lapful of light

1/5/14

(first snow of the season & already I'm missing you,
        Minneapolis)

BOYS WITH FEELINGS on Lowry Hill Liquors' worn brick
It's been the eighties my whole life.

At the museum with my students
I saw a nude who reminded me of you, how powerfully he

swayed back from those hips where flowered

the firm or dozing, dowsing cock. Go on—I am always
    in mind of you; let me

"turn to each other" "I turned to each other" "turned to each

other" . . . this leaves so little to the political imagination (sigh)   Juliana Spahr

(eyes his profile on the pillow—finds the
familiar outline but are his
eyes open or closed)

5/14/12   Last night it happened again.
            Sleep breath but your hands awake
            smooth muscle ripples up to bring
            sternum to sternum in involuntary answer.

            Little work, interlock of good sex, licked a stamen's curl.

            Distant thunder burns through the dead window.

Swensen on   Collaborative voice collects their mutual tendencies so each own
the Waldrops   work can stay more own
at AWP
            Collaboration allows us to express/expel a well-known other

            Dear spirit, what shall I do with my life?
            Came back from the well: What shall I do with my death?

3   Minneapolis, Minnesota

fall 2012 to 6/28/13

Sally Mann's almost too-beautiful
things that let themselves
be seen—even a dead man, body laid at woods' edge, his half-
    gone face
half-turns to her.

I note another thought to look forward to.

"They were mostly ink, brush, wash; grays, blacks, bronzes"   *Eva Hesse*
                                                                Drawing, ed.
                                                                Catherine de
I'm always seeking a haunting   Zegher

That was someone's husband.

I want, as always, more. Turning your face to me
when I say whatever trivial thing I say so that you will

turn to me—oh it's the beginning of fear: ordinary life.

9/10/12

G. E. Lessing
quoted in
Daniel
Tiffany,
Infidel Poetics
"in poetry a garment is not a garment, it conceals nothing"

I lie on my couch after ballet class reading
a vanished world. Want to keep, to make
a record of the present

neither muscular nor spare (fuck your
military aesthetic)

say how her spine centers the ocean in its cursive ah

dark girl in a fluorescent scarf, you're so beautiful
today.

to read   *AVA, Ada,* either ardent life
A Problem from Hell
Cecilia Vicuña

Would I ever tell it as a story?
What if I just write it? Would you know?

exercise: write a letter related to (explaining) each one.

How do you deal with the casual atrocity of the world? Can I
drop into a poem Mankato's mass execution: sitting at the   1862
strip mall coffee shop it comes up,

someone else's catastrophe background for me
my catastrophe, I don't want to censor, I want to admit

how other suffering in this pitiable state of the world
borders a love affair, haze of your
burning village on the horizon of my life—
I don't know.

I know it's not polite to stare but love you look like you've been
walking in this rain a hundred years.

"everyday love, personal ambition and daily worries   Artaud
        are worthless except in relation to
the kind of awful lyricism that exists in those Myths
to which the great mass of men have consented"

"She wanted to be free to do whatever / and a lot of that
        was sexual"
(The New Monogamy)

Hold hands with the cold front coming in.

Make a list of essays I want to write

Thinking about writing to C.,
Dear friend, no, you really didn't know
what I was going through, it was different for me, I couldn't just
hang on to the cliff's edge
like Wile E. Coyote.

For one thing, we didn't love each other. For another,

(acre of lemon trees)
I loved someone else.

Didn't you notice?

A wife agrees. A wife agrees to conceal. She conceals a story.
    But the story swells inside her.

Can I express anger without doing only that?
But why not do that?

She doesn't know, she's never loved a man like you.

Loft a wrist. heft of lost self.
a sheaf of what wheat.

What did he mean by that?

It's only to be expected: pick a fight the day you come back—
well, at least I can scramble eggs,
& everything else you love—right? Isn't that how you really feel,
then the kitchen explodes, oh no
to say goodbye to someone I love & someone I never thought I
would have to say goodbye to,

I'm trying, that is I'm trying to make it clear to you,
I'm done with the river.

How my writing changed when I   10/16/12
began to need it.

"the lyric I—   Adorno,
    that is, the sound of an individuated self,   "Lyric Poetry
    in all its privacy, individuality, & autonomy—is   and Society,"
    always an excision."   quoted in
                                                  Maggie Nelson

Yesterday I told you what I was thinking
promised myself I wouldn't.

a perfect self-expression will move society forward   Hegel
assuming you're not inwardly ugly?

One word & there was permanent neural damage.
That's how love is.

"dear you insufferable cunt"   Kara Walker

Banteay Srei

Her pink temple swept freshly free, the apsara's astral curves swing
under strange eyes. The land mine orchestra plays their
arsenal of leaves.

Land mines don't belong in my work. What do I know about that?

Every few years you grow a new limb where the old one hung
    like a withered flower.

Things I know now, things embryonic and as yet unknown,
universe by heart, any one star a waste of light, washed away in
    say the whole

Orion nebula, a ferry overturns by the island of Lampedusa.

This is not the same, this is radically different,

Lampedusa is a beautiful name
but I should never mention it.

Perhaps it means rock or lantern or oyster

Dear Bernadette,
Keeping a journal on the weather didn't do a thing about
my not loving my husband. I didn't get a single poem
from that stupid list of "flowers I saw today"

"I don't mind where I live, I mind how I live & with whom.
I was terrorized (but didn't know it)
I am, still, terrorized"

Matrimony,
blank as house paint. Tried about sixteen shades of gray green.

Say she paid into those improvements too
then walked away without a cent; say that & say
still people blamed her—why then that's marriage.

Cunts.

color-code problems instead of progress?

some of these I just don't want to go further with. either they're
    done or they're over—no
return.

How many weeks of teaching leave me weary—
they learn nothing &
don't even know what they are supposed to learn and

Dogwood
Coffee,
Calhoun
Square Trying to hear that song I loved above the buzz
but these days you can hear whatever you want whenever you
    want to hear it.

I'm tired of playing the world. Answer back?

Today's savage young gents adore "Phil" Levine.
"Sick line break, bro."

Snow as metaphor for everything
lower than the predicted low

in this my last February of loving you
here (a rhyme begun in one
poem may be landed in a later one).

?   "Don't you think everyone wants to make art that changes the
    world?"

If it doesn't work, lower your standards,
lower them until you can climb over.

A book of poems that begins with a map.   2/6/13 at home

Writing thin enough that you see through it—
you have light to see.

Dear former glacier,

I don't know that this business of being   2/7/13 Lucia's
not a coherent consciousness makes one any happier.
So many things not to believe in.

Feelings Are Facts   to read

"And truth is less a relationship between representation and   Danto
    reality
than a force that keeps the tapestry from unraveling."

Tell me your dreams. No, I mean your personal dreams.   2/8/ *later*

Listen: that's your very own voice singing these strange words.

A book of poems that begins with a nap.

Make it easy, love, oh make it easier on me.

overheard   "you get lovely, very lovely" "it's getting lovelier."
"ever since I left school I feel more lovely than before."

keep typing *lovely* when I mean *lonely*

Cut tangles on revision.

Danto   "For facts correspond to sentences, and when we understand a
sentence,
we understand what fact would make it true." ?

"For the presence or absence of giraffes cannot be
a philosophical difference."
?

"as a set of symptoms of the wayward intellect"
Yes

3/25/13   You look nude uncovered from your book. Dreaming in work,
wild.

What if my life ceases to change? Then I'll have to change it.

Paper tiger.

I traffic in some not quite outdated notions
under domes cobwebbed & cracked. I know it but her saying
    so hit the steel wall inside my
pin skull. Gray sideswipes me. "Sorry." Lofts her backpack,
    gets off.

on the bus
home after
ballet

Sunlight coming through the window is somehow the world.
A student's still talking, tune in.
It's Argo from Chicago.

4/4/13

I'm always asking questions like I'm four years old—
must drive everyone crazy.

There's something to be written I'm not writing
b/c I'm talking

and if you think you're teaching,
you're merely avoiding learning.

Okay—let silence happen then.

How it's hardly ever what you think you want.

I love you & I love sex with you but each time
is only reaching towards something larger.

Ford Parkway
Bridge

Today I saw more people than ever holding signs—
"anything helps,"
"little Demerius died two months ago,"
"are you even nice?"

The Hittites, what became of them
their songs orchards swaddlings

Went for a walk
in a now-vanished world—
heavy snow coats the lake in glacier lace.

Some things you save because you know better.
Some things you save because you love.

It's all aesthetic, i.e., it's all about how plants grow—
which is why some stay open & some are closed, some amper-
    sand, some *and*—

you see I'm not trying to hide anything from you now. Trying
    not to hide.
Your dark hairs everywhere—chestnut, chocolate, black walnut—

not the best fuck ever but we return to dreams which is where
waking up with you again I'm

will never be routine but is

I don't want to know. I am filled with fear. I know, I can't know.

What do you want from your life?
As if *from* your life you could carry it away.

2011, year of miracles.

The cut end curls.

I slept without noticing it. The light's changed. I've gone
already in the beyond. I started this with another
heart. Time's over. I can't remember what I thought I

4   Durham, North Carolina

6/29/13 to summer 2014

TO SEE IT I CLOSED MY EYES

You know better than I do how I look in motion.

This last snow of May
after the long winter
finally we can afford to admire

flocked maples & the ice-calmed sweep of the lake.

It's a placeholder so leave it be.

I am moving, fluttering around the desire—a spoke spinning
　　around one still hub.

Not still, now.

Strung so tight this morning we cannot sit. Move　　　　6/29/13
and take my world with me—you, you on the bed
with the cat, the bed a magic carpet

now jumbled in the back of the rental van
we push to the state line & on.

Magnolias—now I see them
the way I never thought I'd see them
again: in bloom

Lingerie drying on the line storm-caught &
blown high in sweet gum, torn open over
power lines

Acres of aurora borealis—that was the dream—
on the morning we left Minnesota.

Oh I know it's sentimental, I'll take it out later.

Zurita lines bulldozed into the earth / or written in the sky

trumpet vine marks the limit of post-industrial understructure

—ghosts need something solid to build a haunt on

because it blossoms where it can. It can.

Carolina make me as blue as I need to be.

? secondhand "a poem is that in which something that cannot be uncovered
lives"

Your sublunar murmur woke me. Can't be sure ever.

White shirt billows. Walks
diagonally, aslant shoulders, makes a peace sign with
two fingers or, raised to his lips, cunt licking.

Looking out at a blue dumpster. I haven't started to work. 9/13/13
No, I already quit. "They're all phonies. Phonies!"
    says the dream.

Don't want to be
"prematurely middle-aged like an asst prof at some cow college" Sontag

One week and I get paid. Put down seven truths and call it a
    poem. Lifts
a hand as if to bring herself fresh flowers—from

Lee, who can see
that a marigold's chivalric leaf
is prettier than its bitter flower.

The little girl plays at being a little girl.

"I'm going back to my Ph.D." overheard
like "I'm going back to my ex" at Cocoa
    Cinnamon

but I belong, still, to myself—I keep separating myself from
    what I do
for a living, for $300 a month.

The "project" refuses to explain itself. Make notes.

Built on slave labor so it's good to feel bad.

How will she bike home with her coffee in one hand?
That's her problem. What's yours.

My student mentions suicide. Do you have any
idea how much paperwork you've let me in for

Eva Hesse   "small objects strewn together
Drawing   made of latex, wax, fiberglass, & plastic look
                like a placental graveyard"

at MLA   aleatory / discursive / facture / site / essential
          tremor / archive? / *turn*

(nobody hurt in the writing of this poem)

with an upward loop like a lowercase *l* or a hook to the left
    like an Old English *thorn*

Okay, now it's time to circle back
as if with any method you could make it safe!
Childproof the South
or my bitter mind.

How do I make this world yield what I need to get from it?

Get a job so
I can have a
baby. Get a job
with maternity leave oh.

This morning's rejection. Evidence I (carelessly) hurt someone else.

Someone else deserved it!

Start over.

? 10/24/13

The meter maid prints a ticket and crosses the street.

Coupled up, walking lopsided as if we mate for life.

Your father, with a cold & first thing in the morning, rumbles
on the phone to your sister in the city, his voice even deeper
    than yours.

The stolen page hums in the thief's hand.

Get rid of things, but not as paroxysm. On a schedule,
    regularly, shoveling it out.

It's a matter of this: make what you can't forget. It's not that hard
to be perfect.

52

Alice Notley "Why shouldn't a 'person' speak?"

to research   anatomy
the present (in science/philosophy)
letters & diaries
love poems/stories

No.

Henry James "in old, faded ink, and in the most beautiful hand"

of a sudden someone's blue eyes fixed on mine with lust
that's usual
that's the cave
I'm the cave.

(undated note)

So.

don't know / can't compare
stories
moss
mosses grasses
palms are the same ancient thing
getting dressed
sigh.

"coming from the 'battlefield' not the deep
Johannes   psychology or soul"
Göransson

It's not as it should be—
these fragments etc.

The form grows limbs.

Lee's left an orchid in the bathroom window today. You are 1/29/14 CC
sacred to me, absolutely. Of each rib I am enamored.

Will I ever again have the confidence to reject anything out
    of hand?

The faces of students—sometimes people I could have liked
or known, or been friends with.

don't be an *example* / the world is changing

variegated upright streak of amaryllis
(I was a hundred years crossing the Cumberland Gap)

Find out what you want as reader or traveler.
this maze of second thoughts. Translate my needs

my blue jean leg next to yours. I'll be sweet today. Take care
    of me. The last thing
I'd want to do is wear out your love.

Oh god.

It's a long time to be in that hard place.

A more creative life—
postcards to Cindra,

salons, house readings, in-progress showings, pseudo-dance
works in the dark with your hands.

Embroider the ruined sweater. Bring the baby. It doesn't have
to cost money!

Will it end war? feed the hungry? shelter the poor?
undo Jim Crow? make anyone better or wiser?

No, I'm only trying
to communicate something to myself—some cause or weather.

Her hair stained just barely green, as if she's been
swimming in an underground pool for years.

Devon asked me, "How do you make art deep?" Misdirection, 3/6/14
  said I.

In the new world, I'll give one word answers,
I'll be your pythia offering a cryptic puff of smoke.

If I have to be careerist let it not be in poetry at least!

I have to be careerist.

I-40 (news on) barrels around invisible Raleigh,
exit for Lake Wheeler Road—fog lifts over the mill,
little cemetery next door to a trampoline . . . then the
    strawberry farm—

blank plastic hills in February, a green fuzz in March,
but by April when my last maybe has failed the final
ripens a pint of berries to take home.

Sitting and forgetting in the open door. 4/29/14 CC
With the collar of your black leather blazer turned up

& a neatly trimmed beard, damn you're hot but you're not
getting me one dime closer to cheesecake.

What Would Bartleby Do?

If it doesn't work you can do whatever you want to make it work
Think whatever you have to think to get off.

what a lot of people want
from lit is a connection with the author; thus
for my students it's more
important that Emily be a good woman than a good poet

5/2/14   Are you happy with me? You say yes;

your companion weight stays with me all day,
sun like a hand at the back of my neck cradling,
a heavy thumb petting the fontanel.

Go over a copy by hand

crushed, hurrying, passing onwards

music terms   at the bridge—*al niente*: to nothing, fade out—*appassionato*

lissome—necessary—illicit thrill of
double letters

(trying to finish this poem but behind me white people talk
    about "the protests")
I should just start applying for jobs. Anything that's not teaching.

"She came back to borrow a black dress of mine, a beautiful dress"   Sontag
which vanished entirely as she sheathed herself in it.

Get on with forgetting your bad self,

rising on one elbow in a shallow tide
to ask for more. Marred in my instinctual side,

I said the hurtful thing & it went like lightning in your eyes
—your eyes that once were brown but now are green.

Persistent dreams: my dead grandmother, me furious at my ex.

You as a grazing horse.

These barely visible leaves in morning mist—
another word for absence, one absence

in particular. Shiver & shake it off. You don't understand,
    it's okay, you don't need to.

I want to throw it all away, that's how it feels. A hell
full of people I know, that's a real hell, it's okay,

I wanted to quit that job anyway. But I need the fucking money!

x
x
a possible blossom,

My life in the records others kept. How I "failed."

Of course I am a great poet

A storm, the power's out—thank god.

No overall rules ever possible
(ha)

Be honest: it makes me ashamed that I'm halfway to seventy &
    I can't
earn enough to have a child—maternity care
isn't covered on my current insurance

I hate things that reference A. I absolutely cannot. there's no
    poetry—
I feel angrier than ever,

another wave of anger, & I don't even want
to talk about it with myself.

If I can't reshape my experience for good is that a failure on my
    part?

My fertility exceeds its opportunity. We want to,
    but young people
today cannot find work; young people want to work, to find
what immediately you can put your hand to.
A patch of weeds. Pluck it up.
Cradle wind. The cat is making up his mind.

Is this what they mean by *archive*? What self-editing duty, if any,
do I have? Self-police.

I will remove all the cartilage so the joint folds up smaller.

I will take out all the certainty.

well? have you found more here? are you rewarded for your
persistence?

to do   ask Pete about the Poetry Working Group (ok)

I don't know how I feel about crit now. Maybe that's
something I did.

nothing obligatory
sadness of a finished poem

I saw this or that blooming today, I did
this or that, I

saw the sky a bit, bees burying themselves in heather bells.

(delphinium; red salvia; sunflowers in the median
picked apart by goldfinches)

A "concept." Ugh. A "poetry world" a "conpo" a "praxis" a
huh?

Correction: a limitless force.

On stage she's walking a long way
toward a prairie sky projected on the cyc.

More beautiful than her pretty sister.

How useless is what you don't want at the moment?
Prosthetic hand in an antique store.

Armand nabs the one open space at the table   5/19/14 CC

Yes, I am the best possible version of myself, I am
ready to feel pleasure in pleasure & pain in pain.

Darling's intent
No one's paying any attention

Tell me you still need me Reader.
As much as I ever did

Wednesday: write. yoga. make a good dinner.
(sear the little peppers)

There's that woman who looks like Alison M. from one side.

Then a conversation that degrades
into knee contact & a shared sigh (clouds unseen)

but why is the weather here? What does atmosphere matter
to the history of love

Sontag   All "artist as representative sufferer,"
all the nothing I could ever say

to Joyia, having read what Thomas Jefferson
had to say about black people
but those beautiful words—we repeat
hallowed by ancestor believers: WE HOLD

Pollen comes off pine trees in a ghost.

No, that's not right. Start over.

This summer—we'll make it through. Just one month with no
    money
and we can bridge that.

A beautiful sound, the beginning of anyone's name.

The space between
the moment you know it's really you
they're calling.

Someone's twenty-nine-year-old son
slipped off a road in Winona into black water
under ice.

"You can't go from someone else's problems. It's just not right."　　Marina
　　　　　　　　　　　　　　　　　　　　　　　　　　　　　　　Abramović

But Marina, that means I have to
keep having my own problems.

What are you but passage, stranger? Be passage with me.

5   Durham, North Carolina

summer 2014 to –

Acre of silence. A hundred years of waiting—I wasn't
asleep the whole time.

Without the condom
feel an animal
go on need
I want you rude
into me unheld.

First person: art space. Evolution/destruction of art space.   Dance notes
    SABA, the
Southern, Space Space. PS 122.
I'm interested in keeping records: how people
behave, speak, think, live to make. What they wear. How they
    deal.

(More & more this was written in North Carolina not the far
    north)

If I work nearby what can I put my hand to. Tapping maple. I
    don't want
to do nothing, the usual work that can't be seen, make nothing
    for you.

Hopkins   nothing, charged with something
          "will shine out like shook foil"
          a ghost charged with former life
          . . . a something charged with

          when my grandmother died
          felt the shock of transfer. —unfinished. When
          I finish it, will it be dead to me?

7/20/14   With a note signed *Love* you can do whatever you want
          want to fuck me

          maybe I haven't gotten the in-between music right.

          Or am I remembering something else?
          Does that happen to you?

          I haven't been keeping track, am I pregnant?

I contain no one; my insides touch each other, all self
    all the way through.
Self, but bacteria. I feel a bit beat down this Sunday morning.
    Move me, make me
a wild ache of trillium in the woods.

I feel young, but I know better—
my ovaries not pink & smooth
like my other organs but by now
gray & scarred. Pocked

mesh of a fold of flesh,
beach on which a great stone, then a tree, then a body washes up.

Ever will build around—bit of grit, be a pearl.

He had a headache, then a tumor. It's pretty hard to understand,
but when you remove part of a person's brain,

dark blotty ashy. Put a point there. Dreams through which
    time has dripped, erosion,
text warped with honey, leaves stuck together,
a letter transferred.

Reading at
Caffè Driade

The First Flag

Speck of light. Dream
of your pressing bulge. Prow.
Nursed on blood nocturne.

What is happening inside me. I can form
an idea about the fact of secret growth. Geode. It's early days,
nothing's happening, I feel nothing.

Fuck me again, I feel it slipping.

Tending to make the same error at the same place on each page
the nipple cracks and grows, the areola fades

Return it to the dark fold of the lung
where everything waits to be said.

Will I simply gradually delete everything

am a seething dream to some

I want to have a baby without being
infantilized myself. Accept that I will buy a
baby gate socket guard phthalate-free plastic rattle & the like &
    have all necessary etc
because I do for the cat. Aesthetics of cat things don't bother
me invisible to me. I'm writing like Sontag. Who
had her baby early.

Delete the catharsis.

Do you need it? Yes of course. But do you deserve it?

Black salt latte in the modern, well-lit, spacious
pleasure-dome. Everyone wants to be here, away from everything
real.

(your hand grows its bones grasping for me
I a slippery bladder give no purchase as yet)

"memorize a passage of erotic verse"

some guy in
grad school

You are writing prose. Admit it. Where is your ecstatic word?
Like a glimpse of his glans.

I keep learning the thing I forgot
how can it be different always? The poem I can't write persists.

My debts mount, the city changes, my parents age.
In the water by the pier I saw & keep seeing

endless cities of blue sinking,
ultramarine slicked on aqua like weather on mountains which
    is how

you know all your metaphors are wrong.
Now, what can you make from nothing?

21 Winter Projects by Harriet Bart
"Be joyful though you have considered all the facts."
(red silk, moss, gold leaf, eggshell)

I have considered the Islamic State, the coming plague, every scar
on these willow oak trees.

Still I bring forth
from my underground pool.

Should the precious thing be broken with use or love?
Use, or love.

She poked two holes in the shell and blew.

I sleep through it: an hour's molten
gold pours down my hair, nestles in a joining curve.

Have ten minutes to make a little thing that lives.
I'm a smudge. Nerve, marrow smear, & mind.

The sound of downtown Durham
is the sound of construction—the SUNTRUST building
    RUST now.

A blonde girl's hair swings like a flag. It's clearly natural
(just make seven lines, just make enough)

    my girl will have brown hair, your eyes. Dirty pony, flax,
        driftwood. Donna says

"dang" in her NC accent broad as Saturday morning & Libby

    looks down always because she has a toddler trailing

Have ten minutes
have ten years.

Had a premonition of my grandmother's death. Woke & she's   9/30/10
    dead.

No premonition last night

She's been dead.   10/1/14
If I can measure this more precisely perhaps I should because
    that is use.

Find the least promising
artifact & rebuild the body from there: one cracked metatarsal
or a single pearl button.

In films the destruction of the world makes no difference
if someone's saved. So you see
landmark after landmark toppled, loving it.

But no one is saved & the world is destroyed

drawing a house with your (our) little son   6/x/x

Then there was that other child I gave away.
I was sixteen, I dreamed it all.

Grow up & feel
a pulse like yours
stir in one's cunt.

Break up with your family.

Sontag   "Novel about thinking"

I'm thinking of that point in space from which you almost
don't begin,

10/29/x   what the hearts wants.
Libby smiles at the children (Libby is seven months pregnant
I am three)

Are you wanting me to turn to talk to you?

Chunmei, I hope you know when you write your thoughts
    you're not alone

so I told my distant student—sometimes I felt
& sometimes I hated them,

"policing the borders   etc.
of what is a person"

where you begin to belong to me & my curve leans against or
    flows into this answering curve
of you. Not a rule: allure.
So were we lost.

Bones knit
already ever so slightly awry, s/he favors
one fist over the other, beating

on the inside of the lid with a little bone flag.

You are the reader I had in mind.

Asked my love how did it feel to see inside the bole. He said,
    "Amazing." Bony little face
not smiling, having been knit together from its own instructions.

Collect ghost materials.

Because of the light.
Because people cross the street without looking.

Lovely women appear before you now in gilt frames.
Or is that solid gold?

It did not, actually, cost me a thing,
despite the stain.

As if I were drawing you, as if I needed to know you by heart,
    heart.
As if you could possibly die.

in pleated mom jeans as if she needs room for her big pussy
this a purely tentative first draft

Waves to me (that toddler) thinking I am waving to him,
which is charming but also the way of a dictator.

"Being an American poet . . . I thought my function was simply   Baraka
    to talk
about everything as if I knew"

Once I thought my mother's miscarriages were my material.

Dreams about trying to find you or make it up to you
wake & search for you beside me (at the foot of the bed Obi

rolls to spill his white belly) going to need a babysitter
going to have all the normal problems.

Dug free from the bury-clothes, you show no wound at all.

The opposite of pain is not pleasure

the opposite of pain is pain: as, entering the new world,
she ate through the red plush of her own womb.

I devour, devour, & leave
nothing but the bone at the back of the bowl.

From this bone will spring
the green ghost, the mortal intervention.

Erase the palace
as I am loved.

With a gesture clearing her hair to one side of her neck she
    sears the air.

Cut free the form with a line.
Scalpel down the limb, then notch. A style. Aesthetic, beautiful,
    but not the way
you think of beautiful.

You think of beautiful. A slick of pages once a woods.
    Someone's burned down
glen now. A book now, a book among many, a
communal salvage, or savagery. A well of shelves & listing—

you lean in, you listen, which makes you shine.

Lustrous reader, read me—
light the lamp of your likeness over the stamp of mine.

AWP So what if a first-gen. American or an immigrant may take the
same stance—
that doesn't redeem *us*. The *us* of this talk is still white people.

Orderly, the kids go up the hill. They are in school/jail.

Behind me the enforced starlessness, mauve city light of
Minneapolis.

I wake to the cat pushing—two headbutts says what's wrong
with you, get up and feed me.

I'm twenty-six thirty-six twelve weeks of sleep

I can't see two lines into the future. Save me

So I wasn't a good teacher, most of the time. Start there.

With the tide going out, it was dangerous to swim. I felt myself
cut under, so rehearsed what I'd heard: parallel the shore as far

as night needs until lights along the beach mark

the last habitable cove of the island, then stroke
for dear life.

It's too late. Hello true being,

hello deep water,

hello love of my life.

Acknowledgments

These poems would not exist in their current form without the example of Susan Sontag's recently published journals, in particular *Reborn: Journals and Notebooks, 1947–1963* (Picador). I am indebted to Sontag, her publisher, and her son David Rieff, whose sensitive and sympathetic edit makes this work available to a common reader.

I am grateful to the curators and workers of the indelible spaces where this book was written, especially Spyhouse (Nicollet and Hennepin locations) and Dogwood in Minneapolis and Cocoa Cinnamon in Durham.

Thanks to the Walker Art Center Archives & Library, which hosted me for a formative residency.

Thanks to the editors and journals who published poems from this project, including the *Antioch Review* (Judith Hall), *Boston Review* (Stefania Heim), *TYPO* (Adam Clay), *Revolver* (Esther Porter), *Diode* (Jeff Lodge), *DIAGRAM* (Ander Monson), *descant* (Alex Lemon), *Locomotive* (Arto Vaun), and the *Denver Quarterly* (Lindsey Drager).

Finally, gratitude to my students. I carry you with me wherever I go.

LITERATURE
is not the same thing as
PUBLISHING

Coffee House Press began as a small letterpress operation in 1972 and has grown into an internationally renowned nonprofit publisher of literary fiction, essay, poetry, and other work that doesn't fit neatly into genre categories.

Coffee House is both a publisher and an arts organization. Through our *Books in Action* program and publications, we've become interdisciplinary collaborators and incubators for new work and audience experiences. Our vision for the future is one where a publisher is a catalyst and connector.

Funder Acknowledgments

Coffee House Press is an internationally renowned independent book publisher and arts nonprofit based in Minneapolis, MN; through its literary publications and *Books in Action* program, Coffee House acts as a catalyst and connector—between authors and readers, ideas and resources, creativity and community, inspiration and action.

Coffee House Press books are made possible through the generous support of grants and donations from corporations, state and federal grant programs, family foundations, and the many individuals who believe in the transformational power of literature. This activity is made possible by the voters of Minnesota through a Minnesota State Arts Board Operating Support grant, thanks to the legislative appropriation from the arts and cultural heritage fund. Coffee House also receives major operating support from the Amazon Literary Partnership, the Jerome Foundation, The McKnight Foundation, Target Foundation, and the National Endowment for the Arts (NEA). To find out more about how NEA grants impact individuals and communities, visit www.arts.gov.

Coffee House Press receives additional support from the Elmer L. & Eleanor J. Andersen Foundation; the David & Mary Anderson Family Foundation; the Buuck Family Foundation; Dorsey & Whitney LLP; Fredrikson & Byron, P.A.; the Fringe Foundation; Kenneth Koch Literary Estate; the Knight Foundation; the Rehael Fund of the Minneapolis Foundation; the Matching Grant Program Fund of the Minneapolis Foundation; Mr. Pancks' Fund in memory of Graham Kimpton; the Schwab Charitable Fund; Schwegman, Lundberg & Woessner, P.A.; the U.S. Bank Foundation; VSA Minnesota for the Metropolitan Regional Arts Council; and the Woessner Freeman Family Foundation in honor of Allan Kornblum.

The Publisher's Circle of Coffee House Press

Publisher's Circle members make significant contributions to Coffee House Press's annual giving campaign. Understanding that a strong financial base is necessary for the press to meet the challenges and opportunities that arise each year, this group plays a crucial part in the success of Coffee House's mission.

Recent Publisher's Circle members include many anonymous donors, Suzanne Allen, Patricia A. Beithon, Bill Berkson & Connie Lewallen, E. Thomas Binger & Rebecca Rand Fund of the Minneapolis Foundation, Robert & Gail Buuck, Claire Casey, Louise Copeland, Jane Dalrymple-Hollo, Ruth Stricker Dayton, Jennifer Kwon Dobbs & Stefan Liess, Mary Ebert & Paul Stembler, Chris Fischbach & Katie Dublinski, Kaywin Feldman & Jim Lutz, Sally French, Jocelyn Hale & Glenn Miller, the Rehael Fund-Roger Hale/Nor Hall of the Minneapolis Foundation, Randy Hartten & Ron Lotz, Dylan Hicks & Nina Hale, Jeffrey Hom, Carl & Heidi Horsch, Amy L. Hubbard & Geoffrey J. Kehoe Fund, Kenneth Kahn & Susan Dicker, Stephen & Isabel Keating, Kenneth Koch Literary Estate, Allan & Cinda Kornblum, Leslie Larson Maheras, Lenfestey Family Foundation, Sarah Lutman & Rob Rudolph, the Carol & Aaron Mack Charitable Fund of the Minneapolis Foundation, George & Olga Mack, Joshua Mack & Ron Warren, Gillian McCain, Mary & Malcolm McDermid, Sjur Midness & Briar Andresen, Maureen Millea Smith & Daniel Smith, Peter Nelson & Jennifer Swenson, Marc Porter & James Hennessy, Enrique Olivarez, Jr. & Jennifer Komar, Alan Polsky, Robin Preble, Jeffrey Scherer, Jeffrey Sugerman & Sarah Schultz, Alexis Scott, Nan G. & Stephen C. Swid, Patricia Tilton, Stu Wilson & Melissa Barker, Warren D. Woessner & Iris C. Freeman, Margaret Wurtele, Joanne Von Blon, and Wayne P. Zink & Christopher Schout.

For more information about the Publisher's Circle and other ways to support Coffee House Press books, authors, and activities, please visit www.coffeehousepress.org/support or contact us at info@coffeehousepress.org.

Thousands was designed by
Bookmobile Design & Digital Publisher Services.
Text is set in Adobe Garamond Pro.